Compiled by Peter Whitehead & Robin Bean

French Translation by Marie-Claude Apcher

German Translation by Vreni Oleram

Published by Lorrimer Films Ltd., 18 Carlisle St., London, W.1

Designed by Peter Whitehead.

Manufactured and Printed in Gt. Britain
by David Osler & Frank Ltd

CONTENTS

Acknowledgements:

AS YOU LIKE IT—Inter-Allied Film Producers Ltd. **HENRY V**—Rank Film Distributors Ltd. **HAMLET**—Two Cities Film for J. Arthur Rank Organisation. **RICHARD III**—London Films, Laurence Olivier Productions, & Independent Film Distributors Ltd. **OTHELLO**—a BHE Presentation released in the United Kingdom through Eagle Films Ltd.

The British Film Institute & Theo Cowan Ltd.

"We consider it important to preserve and enhance this Othello and more or less present it as one might have seen it at the National Theatre. It was most important for us to preserve the essence of the performance and also to re-create the absolute magic of the theatre on this occasion. In fact, we have put the best cinema resources at the services of great theatre, and will enable millions of people throughout the world who would not have had the remotest chance of seeing Sir Laurence on the stage, to share the experience."

This statement was made by Anthony Havelock-Allan, one of the producers of the film version of **Othello**. Olivier's portrayal of Othello (on the stage) has been regarded by many as one of the greatest experiences in the history of the theatre, and the film itself is intended more as a record of this impressive performance than as a visual treatment of Shakespeare's tragedy. (A sad reflection on the British film industry is that it takes a fantastic success in another medium to enable Olivier's Othello to be brought to the screen.)

Olivier, without question, is regarded as the finest actor in Britain, and possibly the greatest living actor in the world today. And the most respected. Other actors regard it as an honour to work with him; directors find their reputations considerably enhanced when he works with them. His range of roles has been incredibly versatile. In the last few years he has mainly been associated with forceful dynamic roles, whereas earlier in his career he had played romantic leads, in comedy, crime stories and melodrama. And recently he was seen in Preminger's **Bunny Lake is Missing**, as the quietly perceptive police inspector. Yet probably he is most closely associated with his Shakespearean roles and this book is intended as a photographic record of his five Shakespearean interpretations on film (three of which he directed himself): **As You Like It, Henry V, Hamlet, Richard III and Othello.**

Laurence Olivier was born at Dorking, in Surrey, on May 22, 1907. His father, the Rev. Gerald Kerr Olivier, later became vicar of St. Saviour's Church, Pimlico, London, before finally settling in Buckinghamshire. It was while Olivier was a pupil at All Saints' Choir School in London that he became interested in acting. He played Brutus in

Julius Caesar at the age of ten and his performance in the small school auditorium was seen by two of the most prominent personalities of the British theatre, Ellen Terry and Sybil Thorndike. Ellen Terry was also impressed by the performance later as Katharina in **The Taming of the Shrew** which the school presented in 1922 at the Old Shakespearean Theatre in Stratford-upon-Avon. When he completed his education at St. Edward's School in Oxford, Olivier applied for and won a scholarship to London's Central School of Speech Training and Dramatic Art, and it was again in a Shakespeare play that he was singled out for special attention when he won the year's 'best actor' award for **The Merchant of Venice**. Also in the cast was Peggy Ashcroft.

After graduating from the Central School, Olivier's first job was with the Birmingham Repertory Theatre, where he was soon playing major roles in their productions. He was cast in the lead in **Bird in Hand,** again playing opposite Peggy Ashcroft. The repertory group took over London's Royal Court Theatre for a season. Olivier impressed the London critics with his performance in a small American role in Elmer Rice's **The Adding Machine,** and then in **Back to Methuselah** with Cedric Hardwicke and Edith Evans, and in the title role in Tennyson's blank verse play, **Harold.** He remained in London for a seven month run in **Bird in Hand,** and was then offered two plays to follow this, R. C. Sheriff's **Journey's End** (Sheriff was then an unknown amateur actor) and **Beau Geste.** He decided to choose the latter play, which ironically had a brief run, while **Journey's End** became a great success. Fate, for a while, worked against Olivier, and he found himself in one flop after another, but his bad luck came to an end when Noel Coward asked him to play Victor Prynne opposite Gertrude Lawrence and Coward himself in his new comedy **Private Lives.** The play was a great success and later transferred to Broadway with the same cast. He was approached by Hollywood companies to make films on the West Coast, but for two years was given uninspiring parts, and he returned to London, very disillusioned with film-making.

In England he played with Gloria Swanson in the film **Perfect Understanding,** and then returned to the West End stage to appear in **The Rats of Norway** with Raymond Massey and Gladys Cooper. He returned to Hollywood when he was asked to play opposite Garbo in **Queen Christine**, but found himself replaced by John Gilbert. This made him turn his back on films for some time, and he determined to concentrate on the theatre.

He received high critical praise when he appeared on Broadway in **The Green Bay Tree**, then he played in London in Noel Coward's production of **Biography,** with Ina Claire. He played Bothwell in **Mary, Queen of Scots** in which he first worked with John Gielgud. In Noel Coward's presentation of the American satire based on the Barrymore family, Olivier played the flamboyant role of matinee idol 'Tony Cavendish' with such verve that he broke his ankle one night leaping from a balcony. In **The Ringmaster** he played a neurotic cripple who was master-minding a crime ring.

Alexander Korda, the Hungarian director-producer who became one of the most important film-makers in Britain, persuaded Olivier to set aside his prejudices against films and to agree to sign a contract with Korda's company, London Films, which was lining up an impressive production programme. Olivier also went into theatre management for the first time, with **Golden Arrow** in which he played with Greer Garson. But he gained his greatest recognition when John Gielgud, who was producing **Romeo and Juliet** (1935), decided to step out of the part of Romeo for the first six weeks of the run and asked Olivier to take over. For the remainder of the run, he alternated with Gielgud as Mercutio. In 1937 Tyrone Guthrie invited him to play the title role in a new full length version of Hamlet at the Old Vic. After this Olivier stayed at the Old Vic for two years during which time he appeared as Macbeth, Henry V, Sir Toby Belch, Iago and Coriolanus.

After this he was approached by producer Sam Goldwyn and director William Wyler to play Heathcliff in an adaptation of Emily Bronte's **Wuthering Heights** with Merle Oberon. His screen career now took on a more positive line, and he next took the part of Max de Wynter in Alfred Hitchcock's adaptation of Daphne du Maurier's **Rebecca,** and then Mr. Darcy in the film of Jane Austen's **Pride and Prejudice.** By now World War II had begun and he was training as a pilot for the Fleet Air Arm. But before his acceptance for this he played a French-Canadian trapper in **49th Parallel.** While in the service he obtained temporary leave to star in Anthony Asquith's **Demi Paradise,** a satire about a Russian engineer's involvement with the English middle class in pre-war Britain. He later received leave for the filming of **Henry V,** which was set up by Felipe del Guidice. Laurence Olivier for this film undertook the mammoth task of producing, directing and playing the title role in what was his second venture into Shakespeare on screen (he had previously appeared with Elizabeth Bergner in Czinner's **As You Like It** in 1936). Locations were filmed in Ireland and for long tracking shots Olivier built his own railway. The film ran for eleven months in London, and Olivier received a special Academy Award for his triple capacity of producer, director and star. He said of the part of Henry that 'the difficulty in Henry's character is its complete straightforwardness'.

The Old Vic Theatre Company had ceased to be active after the theatre was destroyed during the Blitz, but in 1944 Olivier, together with Ralph Richardson, Tyrone Guthrie and John Burrell, reformed the company which re-opened at another London theatre, the New Theatre. During the first season Olivier played Sergius in **Arms and the Man,** the title role in **Richard III** and Astrov in **Uncle Vanya.** The next season he played Hotspur and Shallow in **Henry IV** Parts One and Two, Oedipus in **Oedipus Rex** and Mr. Puff in **The Critic.** The last two were performed as a double bill, which in April 1946 he took to New York. Later that year he returned to London to star in his own production of **King Lear.**

Early in 1947, Olivier began work on his screen version of **Hamlet** which, like **Henry V,** he produced and directed as well as playing the title role. He described this film as 'an essay in **Hamlet**—the tragedy of a man who could not make up his mind'.

'When I was making **Henry V** I had thought about a film of **Hamlet** but had not followed up the idea in any detailed way. When the question of a second Shakespearean film came up, however, **Hamlet** seemed the obvious choice. From my own experience on **Henry V,** I had learnt that in dealing with Hamlet the only real way to solve the problem of adaptation for the screen was to be ruthlessly bold in adapting the original play. I find it very difficult to pin down how and when I first conceived the basic idea for the treatment of the film **Hamlet.** Quite suddenly, one day, I visualised the final shot of **Hamlet.** And from this glimpse, I saw how the whole conception of the film could be built up'. He edited the play, which in its full version runs for four and a half hours, down to a film of two and a half hours, and took out the characters of Rosencrantz, Guildenstern and Fortinbras, and simplified the story. He felt that the film should be regarded more as 'an "Essay in Hamlet", and not as a film version of a necessarily abridged classic'.

Olivier had his hair dyed, because fair hair fitted his conception of Hamlet. He took infinite care over the shooting of the film, and the ten minute duelling sequence for example took 14 days to shoot. While filming at the Denham Studio he received a Knighthood in the Birthday Honours list, for services to the stage and screen.

Hamlet was described as 'a £475,000 triumph', Olivier's performance was generally agreed to be magnificent, and the film was awarded Best Foreign Film prize at the 1948 Venice Festival, as well as winning five Oscars including that for best film of the year and for Best Actor.

In 1948 Olivier took the Old Vic Company on a tour to Australia and New Zealand with **Richard III, The Skin of Our Teeth** and **School for Scandal.** He then produced several plays for his own company, Laurence Olivier Productions, beginning with **Born Yesterday.** In order to carry out his long-term plans as actor-manager he acquired the lease of the St. James's Theatre, where he continued his policy of combining experienced actors with talented newcomers. A hitherto unknown actress, Heather Stannard, was acclaimed for her performance opposite Olivier in Christopher Fry's **Venus Observed,** while Peter Finch, whom Olivier had met as a factory entertainer while touring in Australia, first came into the limelight in a Viennese role in **Daphne Laureola.** Other notable Olivier productions at this time included Menotti's Opera **The Consul, Anthony and Cleopatra** (which he also produced in New York), and **The Sleeping Prince,** which a few years later he adapted as a film.

Although so actively engaged in the Theatre, Olivier found time for several films and starred in William Wyler's **Carrie,** and played his first singing role as the handsome, devil-may-care highwayman in **The Beggar's Opera,** the first film to be directed by Peter Brook.

He then spent many months preparing the production of his third Shakespearean film, and in 1954 began work on **Richard III,** again directing, producing and playing the title role, and surrounding himself with an impressive cast which included Ralph Richardson, John Gielgud, Claire Bloom, Cedric Hardwicke, Alec Clunes, and Laurence Naismith. The film was shot in Vistavision and breath-taking battle scenes were filmed in Spain. The film was described as a magnificent achievement for British cinema, and a fine record of a great actor.

Olivier surprised many people with his choice of co-star for his next film, when he imported Marilyn Monroe to play opposite him in his screen adaptation of Rattigan's **The Sleeping Prince**, which was re-titled **The Prince and the Showgirl.** The breakaway from his classical image was followed by another off-beat role when he played the sleasy down-at-heel music hall artist Archie Rice in John Osborne's play **The Entertainer,** which he subsequently played in the film version directed by Tony Richardson, which also featured Albert Finney in a supporting role.

Olivier then tried to raise the necessary £500,000 for a screen version of **Macbeth;** he was offered the money but only on the condition he played on the stage in an adaptation of **Jane Eyre.** Instead, Olivier took on the role of General Burgoyne in the film of Shaw's **The Devil's Disciple,** in which he played opposite Burt Lancaster. Afterwards came his debut on British television, in **John Gabriel Borkman,** but he regards the experience as 'a disaster'. He fared better in his first American television play, **The Moon and Six-pence** which he described as 'not a disaster—it even fetched in a little Oscar'. After that he returned to Hollywood for Stanley Kubrick's epic of political intrigue in Rome, **Spartacus,** in which he acted with Kirk Douglas and Charles Laughton.

Olivier took on something of a physical endurance test, when he combined **Coriolanus** at Stratford-upon-Avon with his appearance before the cameras for **The Entertainer.** He caught up on his sleep in an ambulance travelling between the theatre in Stratford and the North of England locations for the film. He followed this with his appearance on the New York stage in **The Tumbler** and in **Rhinoceros** in London. Also in the same year, 1960, he appeared in New York in the very successful production of **Becket** in which he and Anthony Quinn alternated in the roles of Henry II and Becket. While in New York he appeared in David Susskind's television production of Graham Greene's **The Power**

and the Glory with Julie Harris and George C. Scott, which was shown in the cinemas in Europe.

Returning to England he launched the Chichester Festival Theatre, and then starred in Peter Glenville's film **Term of Trial** with Simone Signoret, Terence Stamp and Sarah Miles.

In August 1962, he took over the directorship of the National Theatre, which opened with his production of **Hamlet,** with Peter O'Toole in the title role. Olivier has contributed greatly to the success of the National Theatre through his own performances in **Othello, Uncle Vanya, The Recruiting Officer** and **The Master Builder.** The company has already toured extensively in England and has visited Moscow and West Berlin, with Olivier's **Othello** as its centrepiece.

1965 proved to be one of the most active years of his career. He was involved with four new productions at the National Theatre: John Arden's **Armstrong's Last Goodnight,** Pinero's **Trelawney of the Wells,** the double bill of Strindberg's **Miss Julie** and Peter Shaffer's **Black Comedy** and Congreve's **Love for Love** in which he played Tattle. As well as this, he made his first film for four years when he rearranged his activities to make time to appear in Otto Preminger's **Bunny Lake is Missing** as the Scotland Yard inspector investigating the mysterious disappearance of a small child in London. In this film he was reunited, after 35 years, with the man responsible for giving him his first crucial break on the London stage, Noel Coward. Also in 1965 the film production of his **Othello** was started, with the original cast from the National Theatre. He describes this as "neither an ordinary film, nor a camera recording of a theatrical presentation."

This he followed with a third film for that year, when he played the fanatical Mahdi in Basil Dearden's **Khartoum,** with Charlton Heston as General Gordon and Ralph Richardson as Gladstone.

"Nous considérons qu'il est important de conserver et de mettre en valeur cet Othello et de le présenter plus ou moins comme on aurait pu le voir au Théâtre National. Il était important pour nous de conserver l'esprit de la présentation et de récréer l'atmosphere magique de la salle du théâtre en cette occasion. En fait, nous avons mis les meilleurs ressources du cinéma aux services du grand théâtre, ce qui permettra à des milliers de personnes par le monde entier, qui n'auraient pu autrement avoir la moindre chance de voir Sir Laurence sur scène, de partager cette expérience."

Ceci a été dit par Anthony Havelock-Allan, un des metteurs en scène de la version cinématographique **d'Othello.** L'interprétation d'Othello par Olivier sur scène est considérée par beaucoup comme une des plus grandes expériences dans l'histoire du théâtre, et l'intention du film lui-même est de présenter un document d'une interprétation impressionnante plutôt qu'un traitement visuel de la tragédie de Shakespeare (ceci est une triste réflection sur l'industrie du film britannique qui a besoin d'une grand succès dans un autre milieu pour permettre l'Othello d'Olivier d'être présenté sur l'ecran.)

Olivier est indiscutablement considéré comme étant le meilleur acteur en Grande Bretagne, et probablement le plus grand acteur vivant du monde entier—ainsi que le plus respecté.

C'est un grand honneur pour un autre acteur de travailler avec lui; les metteurs en scène constatent que leur réputation est considérablement mise en valeur lorsqu'-Olivier travaille avec eux. Son répertoire est d'une variété incroyable. Au cours des dernières années, on l'a principalement associé avec des rôles puissants et dynamiques. Alors qu'au début de sa carrière il avait joué des rôles romantiques ou bien des comédies, des histoires policières ou des mélodrames. On l'a vu récemment dans **Bunny Lake is Missing** de Preminger dans le rôle du tranquille et perspicace inspecteur de police. Toutefois il est sans doute plus souvent identifié avec ses rôles de Shakespeare et l'intention de ce livre est de présenter un document photographique des cinq interprétations shakespeariennes à l'ecran (dont il fut metteur en scène pour trois). **As You Like It, Henry IV, Hamlet, Richard III,** and **Othello.**

Laurence Olivier est né à Dorking, en Surrey, le 22 mai

1907. Son père, le Rev. Gerald Kerr Olivier, devint plus tard Curé de l'Eglise de St. Saviour à Pimlico, Londres, avant de s'établir définitivement dans le département de Buckinghamshire. Ce fut lorsqu'Olivier était élève à l'ecole de Choeur De all Saint à Londres qu'il montra pour la première fois un intérêt pour le théâtre. Il joua dans **Jules Cesar** le rôle de Brutus à l'âge de 10 ans et son interprétation sur la petite scène de l'école fut vue par deux des plus importantes personalités du théâtre britannique, Ellen Terry et Sybil Thorndike.

Ellen Terry fut impressionnée plus tard par son interprétation de Katharina dans **Taming of the Shrew** présenté par son école en 1922 au vieux théâtre de Stratford en Avon. Ayant terminé ses études à l'école de St. Edward à Oxford, Olivier fit une demande pour une bourse à l'école Centrale de Diction et d'Art Dramatique de Londres, qu'il obtint, et ce fut de nouveau dans une piéce de Shakespeare qu'il se fit remarquer lorsqu'il gagna le prix du meilleur acteur de l'année pour son interprétation dans le **Marchand de Venice.** Presentée dans la même pièce était Peggy Ashcroft.

Ayant terminé ses examens à l'Ecole Centrale, la première situation d'Olivier fut avec le Théâtre de Répertoire de Birmingham où il parvint très vite à jouer les rôles principaux de la production. Ce fut lui qui joua le role principal dans **Bird in Hand,** de nouveau avec Peggy Ashcroft. La compagnie de répertoire occupa pour une saison le Théâtre Royal Court à Londres. Olivier impressionna les critiques londoniens avec son interprétation d'un petit rôle américain dans **Adding Machine** d'Elmer Rice, ensuite dans **Back to Methuselah** avec Cedric Hardwicke et Edith Evans et finalement dans le rôle principal **d'Harold,** pièce en vers de Tennyson. Il resta à Londres pour les sept mois que dura **Bird in Hand,** lorsqu'on lui offrit deux pièces, **Journey's End** de R. C. Sheriff (Sheriff était alors un acteur inconnu) et **Beau Geste.** Il décida de choisir cette dernière pièce qui **n'eut** d'ailleurs qu'un bref succès alors que **Journey's End** devint un grand succés. Le sort pour un instant joua contre Olivier et il fit face à une serie d'insuccès, mais sa malchance prit fin lorsque Noel Coward le pria de jouer Victor Prynne avec Gertrude Lawrence et Coward lui-même dans sa nouvelle comédie **Private Lives.** Cette pièce fut un grand succès et fut transférée plus tard à Broadway avec les mêmes actuers. Plusieurs compagnies d'Hollywood lui demandèrent de faire des films sur la côte Ouest mais on lui donna pendant deux ans des rôles sans intérêt et il revint à Londres fort désillusionné avec le cinéma.

En Angleterre il joua avec Gloria Swanson dans le film **Perfect Understanding** et ensuite réapparut sur scène dans le West End pour prendre part à la piece **The Rats of Norway** avec Raymond Massey et Gladys Cooper. Il retourna à Hollywood lorsqu'on lui demanda de jouer avec Greta Garbo dans **Queen Christine** mais s'étant trouvé remplacé par John Gilbert, il tourna le dos au cinéma pendant quelque temps et se consacra au théâtre.

. Il fut l'objet de louanges par les critiques lorsqu'il parut à Broadway dans **The Green Bay Tree** et joua ensuite à Londres dans la production de Noel Coward **Biography** avec Ian Claire. Il joua également Bothwell dans **Mary, Queen of Scots** où il travailla pour la première fois avec John Gielgud. Dans la présentation de Noel Coward du satire américain basé sur la famille Barrymore, Olivier prit le rôle flamboyant de l'idole le l'écran 'Tony Cavendish' qu'il interpréta avec un tel enthousiasme qu'il brisa sa cheville un certain soir en sautant d'une balcon. Dans le **Ring Master** il joua le rôle d'un infirme neurasthénique qui était le chef d'une organisation criminelle.

Alexander Korda, le directeur et metteur en scène hongrois qui devint un des plus importants cinéastes en Grande Bretagne, réussit à convaincre Olivier d'oublier ses préjugés contre le cinéma et de consentir à signer un contrat avec la compagnie de Korda, London Films, qui était en train de préparer un impressionnant programme de production. Olivier se lança également pour la première fois dans la direction théâtrale avec **Golden Arrow** où il joua avec Greer Garson. Il fut le plus apprecié à sa juste valeur lorsque John Gielgud, qui était alors metteur en scène de **Romeo et Juliet** (1935), décida de se retirer du rôle de Romeo pour les six premières semaines de la saison et demanda à Olivier de prendre son rôle. Pendant le restant de la saison, il prit à tour de rôle avec Gielgud le rôle de Mercutio. En 1937, Tyrone Guthrie l'invita à jouer le rôle principal dans une nouvelle version originale de Hamlet au Théâtre du Old Vic. Ensuite Olivier resta avec le théâtre du Old Vic pendant deux ans durant lesquels il joua les rôles de Macbeth, Henry V, Sir Toby Belch, Iago et Coriolanus.

Le metteur en scène Sam Goldwyn et le directeur William Wyler lui offrirent le rôle de Heathcliff dans une adaptation de **Wuthering Heights** d'Emily Bronte avec Merle Oberon. Sa carrière au cinema suivit une direction plus positive à partir de cette époque et il ensuite le rôle de Max de Wynter dans l'adaptation d'Alfred Hitchcock du roman de Daphné du Maurier **'Rebecca'** ainsi que le rôle de M. Bercy dans le film **Pride and Prejudice,** adapté du roman de Jane Austen. A cette époque, la deuxiéme guerre mondiale avait débuté et Olivier suivit un cours d'entrainement comme pilote dans l'aviation marine. Il avait toutefois pu avant ceci jouer le rôle d'un trappeur canadien français dans **49th Parallel.** Pendant son service militaire il obtint une permission temporaire pour jouer le rôle principal dans **Demi Paradise** d'Anthony Asquith, satire d'un ingénieur russe aux prises avec le bourgeoisie anglaise d'avant guerre. Plus tard, il obtint une permission pour le film **d'Henry V** qui fut présenté par Felipe Del Guidice. Pour ce film, Laurence Olivier entreprit la tâche immense de produire, de mettre en scène et de jouer le rôle principal dans son deuxième essai de Shakespeare à l'ecran (il avait précedemment jouer avec Elizabeth Bergner dans **As You Like It** de Czinner en 1936). Les scènes extérieures furent tournées en Irlande et pour certaines scènes sur de longues distances, Olivier construisit son propre chemin de fer. Le film joua pendant 11 mois à Londres et Olivier reçut un prix académique spécial pour son triple rôle de metteur en scène, directeur et étoile. Il a dit de son rôle d'Henry: "la difficulté dans le charactère d'Henry consiste dans son entière droiture".

La **compagnie du théâtre du Old Vic** avait cessé d'exister après la destruction du théâtre durant les bombardements, mais en 1944, Olivier avec Ralph Richardson, Tyrone Guthrie et John Burrell, reforma la compagnie qui fut présentée de nouveau à un autre théâtre londonien, New Theatre. Au cours de la première saison, Olivier joua le rôle de Sergius dans **Arms and the Man,** le rôle principal dans **Richard III** et celui de Astrov dans **Uncle Vanya.** Pendant la seconde saison, il joua le rôle de Hotspur et Shallow dans **Henry IV** Actes I et II, Oedipus dans **Oedipus Rex,** et M. Puff dans The **Critic.** Ces dernières pièces furent présentées sur le même programme et il les joua à New York en Avril 1946. Plus tard dans l'année, il rentra â Londres pour jouer le rôle principal dans sa propre production de **King Lear.**

Au début de 1947, Olivier commença sa version cinématographique de Hamlet qui comme Henry V, fut mise en scène et dirigée par lui même et où il joua également le rôle principal. Il décrivit le film comme étant "un essai sur Hamlet—la tragédie d'un homme incapable de prendre une décision".

"Lorsque je tournais Henry V, j'avais songé à un film sur Hamlet, mais n'avais pas poursuivi cette idée d'aucune façon. Cependant lorsqu'il fut question d'un deuxième film Shakespearien, Hamlet me sembla être le choix évident. D'après ma propre expérience avec Henry V, je m'étais rendu compte qu'en approchant le sujet de Hamlet, la seule façon de résoudre le problème d'une adaptation pour l'écran était d'être impitoyablement téméraire dans l'adaptation de la pièce originale. Il m'est très difficile de préciser quand et comment j'ai conçu pour la première fois l'idée fondamentale du traitement du film Hamlet. Un jour soudain, je vis dans mon esprit la dernière image d'Hamlet. Et de ce vif aperçu, je construis l'entière conception de ce film." Il édita la pièce qui dans sa version entière dure 4h¼ pour la réduire à un film de 3h½, supprima les rôles de Rosencrantz, Guildenstern et Fortinbras et simplifia l'histoire. Il pensait que le film devait être considéré comme 'un essai sur Hamlet' plutôt qu'une version cinématographique d'un classique abrégé.

Olivier se fit teindre les cheveux car une chevelure blonde entrait dans sa conception de Hamlet. Il prit des peines infinies pour tourner le film, par exemple la scène du duel qui dure 10 minutes sur l'écran, lui prit 14 jours à tourner. C'est au cours du tournage au studio de Denham qu'il fut nommé Chevalier sur la liste d'honneur de l'anniversaire de la Reine, pour services rendus au théâtre et à l'écran.

On décrivit Hamlet comme'une triomphe de 475.000 livres', l'interprétation d'Olivier a été généralement acclaimé comme magnifique et le film gagna le prix du meilleur film étranger au Festival de Venice de 1948 et gagna également cinq oscars, y compris celui du meilleur film de l'année et du Meilleur Acteur.

En 1948, Olivier emmena la Compagnie du Old Vic pour une tournée en Australie et Nouvelle Zélande avec Richard III, the Skin of Our Teeth et School for Scandal. Il mit alors en scène plusieurs pièces pour sa propre compagnie, les productions Laurence Olivier, débutant avec **Born Yester-day**. Afin de mettre ses projets à longues échéances comme acteur-directeur à l'execution, il acquis le bail du théâtre de St. James où il poursuivit sa politique de faire jouer des acteurs experimentés avec des nouveaux venus de talent. Jusqu'alors inconnue, Heather Stannard, fut acclaimée pour sa représentation avec Olivier dans **Venus Observed** de Christopher Fry, alors que Peter Finch qui était comédien pour le divertissement d'ouvriers d'usine lorsqu'Olivier le rencontra au cours d'une tournée en Australie se fit remarquer pour la première fois dans un rôle viennois dans **Daphne Laureola**. Olivier eut quelques autres productions remarquables á cette éqoque: L'Opera de Menotti **The Consul, Anthony and Cleopatra** (qu'il mit en scène également à New York) et le **Sleeping Prince** qu'il adapta plus tard pour l'écran.

Bien qu'étant engagé si activement par le théâtre, Olivier trouva néammoins le temps de tourner dans plusieurs film et prit le rôle principal de **Carrie** de William Wyler et joua son premier rôle chantant du voleur de grand chemin insouciant et beau garcon dans le **Beggar's Opera**, le premier film mit en scène par Peter Brook. Il passa ensuite plusieurs mois á préparer la production de son **troisième film et en 1954**, commença Richard III, étant une **fois de plus directeur**, metteur en scène et acteur principal entouré d'une brillante compagnie qui comprenait Ralph Richardson, John Gielgud, Claire Bloom, Cedric Hardwicke, **Alec Clunes**, et Laurence Naismith. Le film fut tourné en vistavision et les scènes impressionnantes des batailles furent tournées en Espagne. Le film a été décrit comme un magnifique exploit du cinéma britannique et un enregistrement de qualité d'un grand acteur.

Beaucoup de personnes furent surprises lorsqu'Olivier choisit comme actrice principale pour son prochain film, Marilyn Monroe, qu'il fit venir pour jouer avec lui dans son **interprétation á l'écran de The Sleeping Prince** qui fut **réintitulé The Prince and the Showgirl**. Cette rupture avec son image classique fut suivie par un autre rôle inhabituel lorsqu'il joua l'artiste minable de Music Hall, Archie Rice, dans la pièce de John Osborne, **The Entertainer**, rôle qu'il reprit plus tard dans la version pour l'écran par Tony Richardson où prit part également l'acteur Albert Finney.

Olivier essaya alors d'obtenir la somme de 500.000

livres necéssaire pour une version cinématographique de Macbeth. L'argent lui fut effectivement offert mais seulement à la condition qu'il prit part á une adaptation pour le théâtre de Jane Eyre. Mais Olivier prit le rôle du General Burgoyne dans le film de Shaw **The Devil's Disciple** où il joua avec Burt Lancaster. Vint ensuite son début à la television dans **John Gabriel Borkman,** mais il considéra cette expérience comme un désastre. Il eut plus de succès dans sa première pièce à la Télévision américaine, **The Moon and Sixpence** qu'il décrivit comme "pas un désastre—j'y ai même gagné un petit Oscar". Il retourna ensuite à Hollywood pour prendre part au film à grand spectacle de Stanley Kubrick d'une intrigue politique à Rome, **Spartacus,** où il joua avec Kirk Douglas et Charles Laughton.

Ce fut un veritable test d'endurance physique lorsque Olivier entreprit de jouer simultanément **Coriolanus** à Stratford en Avon et **The Entertainer** au studio. Il parvint á dormir dans une ambulance qui voyageait entre le théâtre de Stratford en Avon et le nord de l'Angleterre où furent tournées les scènes extérieures du film. Ensuite il parus sur scène à New York dans **The Tumbler** et à Londres dans la pièce le **Rhinoceros.** En 1960, également, il parus à New York dans une production de **Becket** qui obtint un grand succès et où il prit à tour de rôle avec Anthony Quinn les rôles d'Henry II et Becket. C'est à New York qu'il parut dans la production de Susskind pour la télévision, **The Power and the Glory** de Graham Greene, avec Julie Harris et George C. Scott, production qui fut présentée sur l'ecran en Europe.

De retour en Angleterre, il lança le Théâtre Festival de Chichester et prit le rôle principal dans le film de **Term of Trial** avec Simone Signoret, Terence Stamp et Sarah Miles.

En aôut 1962, il prit en main le direction du Théâtre National par ses propres interprétations dans **Othello, Uncle Vanya, The Recruiting Officer** et the **Master Builder.** Cette compagnie a déja fait des tournées importantes en Angleterre et a visité Moscou et Berlin Ouest avec Olivier dans le rôle d'Othello comme pièce principale de son repertoire.

1965 s'est averée être une des années les plus actives de sa carrière. Il s'occupa de quatre nouvelles productions au Théâtre National: **Armstrong's Last Goodnight** de John Arden, **Trelawney of the Wells** de Pinero, le double programme **Miss Julie** de Strindberg et **Black Comedy** de Peter Shaffer, et **Love for Love** où il joua Tattle. Il tourna également dans son premier film depuis quatre ans lorsqu'il réorganisa ses activités afin de paraitre dans le film **Bunny Lake is Missing** d'Otto Preminger dans le rôle de l'inspecteur de Scotland Yard faisant une enquête sur la mystérieuse disparition d'un enfant à Londres. Dans ce film, il retrouva après 35 ans l'homme qui lui avait donné sa première chance sur la scène du théâtre, Noel Coward. Il commença également in 1965, la production cinématographique de son **Othello** avec la troupe originale au Théâtre National. Il a décrit ce film comme étant ni un film ordinaire ni un enregistrement photographique d'une représentation théâtrale.

La même année, il fit un troisième film où il joua le rôle du fanatique Madhi dans **Khartoum** de Basil Dearden avec Charlton Heston qui joua General Gordon et Ralph Richardson qui joua Gladstone.

Bien qu'il soit de plus en plus pris par ses travaux administratifs, il trouve malgré tout le temps, non seulement de découvrir et l'encourager les acteurs et les actrices qui font partie de la compagnie du Théâtre National, mais aussi de surprendre par la puissance et l'originalité qu'il apporte à chaque nouvelle interprétation.

"**Wir glauben, dass es von Bedeutung ist, die Auffuehrung des Othello, wie man sie im National Theatre haette
miterleben koennen, zu erhalten.** Von ganz besonderer
Bedeutung fuer uns war dabei, das Wesen dieser Vorstellung, und damit die Zauberkraft der Buehne, festzuhalten.
Wir haben dafuer die allerbesten Mittel des Films herange-
zogen. **So werden Millionen von Menschen, die sonst
niemals die Gelegenheit gehabt haetten, Sir Laurence auf
der Buehne zu sehen, an diesem Ereignis teilnehmen
koennen".**

Dies sagt Anthony Havellock-Allan, einer der Produzen-
ten des verfilmten **Othello.** Viele betrachten Oliviers
Darstellung von **Othello** (auf der Buehne) als eines der
groessten Ereignisse in der Geschichte des Theaters. Dieser
Film soll seine imposante Leistung aufzeichnen, und nicht
eine filmische Bearbeitung der Tragodie Shakespeares sein.
(Das Oliviers **Othello** zuerst den grossartigen Erfolg auf der
Buehne braucht, um auf der Leinwand moeglich zu werden,
ist eine Tatsache, die der Britischen Film Industrie keine
Ehre macht.)

Ohne Zweifel betrachtet man Olivier als den groessten
Schauspieler Grossbritanniens, vielleicht sogar als den
groessten lebenden Schauspieler der Welt. Auf jeden Fall
ist er der am meisten verehrte. Fuer andere Schauspieler
ist es eine grosse Ehre, mit ihm zu arbeiten, Regisseure
werden beruehmter, wenn er mit ihnen arbeitet. Die Auswahl
seiner Rollen war, und ist, unglaublich vielseitig. In den
letzten Jahren waren es meistens schwingende, dynamische
Auftritte, im Gegensatz zu der Anfangszeit seiner Laufbahn,
da er in einer romantischen Hauptrolle zu sehen war, in
Komoedien, Kriminalstuecken und Melodramen auftrat.
Unlaengst konnte er in Otto Premingers **Bunny Lake is Missing (Bunny Lake Wird Vermisst)** gesehen werden, und zwar
in der Rolle des ruhigen, scharfsichtigen Polizei-Inspektors.
Er ist aber wohl besten fuer seine Shakespearischen Rollen
bekannt, und dieses Buch soll eine Sammlung Photogra-
phien seiner fuenf Shakespearischen Darstellungen im Film
sein (drei davon unter eigener Regie), naemlich **As You
Like It. (Wie es euch gefaellt), Henry V, Hamlet, Richard
III,** und **Othello.**

Laurence Olivier ist am 22. May 1907 in Dorking, Surrey,
geboren. Sein Vater, Reverend Gerald Kerr Oliver, wird

spaeter Pfarrer an der St. Saviour's Kirche, Pimlico, London, bevor er sich in Buckinghamshire niederlaesst. Waehrend seiner Schulzeit in All Saints Choir School (Aller Heiligen Chor Schule) in London erwacht Oliviers Interesse zum Theater. Zehnjaehrig, spielt er Brutus in **Julius Caesar.** Sein Auftritt in dem kleinen Schultheater wird von zwei der groessten Persoenlichkeiten des englischen Theaters gesehen: Ellen Terry und Sybil Thorndike. 1922 spielt die Schule **The Taming of the Shrew (Der Widerspenstigen Zaehmung)** auf der Buehne des Old Shakespearean Theatres in Stratford-upon-Avon, und Olivier Auftritt als Katharina beeindruckt Ellen Terry. Nach weiteren Schuljahren an der St. Edward's Schule in Oxford bewirbt er sich um ein Stipendium fuer die Central School of Speech Training and Dramatic Art. Er erhält es. Wieder ist es ein Shakespeare-Stueck, in welchen er ausgezeichnet wird, und zwar gewinnt er den Jahrespreis fuer den besten Schauspieler fuer seine Leistung in **The Merchant of Venice (Der Kaufmann von Venedig).** Unter den damaligen Kollegen befindet sich auch Peggy Ashcroft. Sein erstes Engagement nach Abschluss ist bei dem Birmingham Repertory Theatre. Er spielt bald Hauptrollen. Neben Peggy Ashcroft spielt er die Hauptrolle in **Bird in Hand (Vogel in der Hand).** Dieses Provinztheater zieht fuer eine Saison nach London ins Royal Court Theatre. Olivier beeindruckt die Londoner Kritiker mit seiner Darstellung von einer kleineren amerikanischen Rolle in Elmer Rice's **The Adding Machine. (Die Additions-Maschine)** und dann in **Back to Methuselah (Zurueck zu Methuselah),** wo er neben Cedrick Hardwicks und Edith Evans spielt, und auch in der Titelrolle in **Harold,** Tennysons Blankversdrama. Sieben Monate bleibt er in London, in dem Stueck **Bird in Hand,** und erhaelt dann zwei weitere Stuecke zur Auswahl angeboten, R. C. Sheriffs' **Journey's End (Der Reise Ende)** (Sheriff war zu der Zeit ein unbekannter Amateur-Schauspieler) und **Beau Geste.** Er waehlt das letztere, welches sich ironischerweise nur kurze Zeit haelt, waehrend **Journey's End** ein grosser Erfolg wird. Das Schicksal schlaegt nun etwas hart zu, Olivier spielt in einen Reinfall nach dem andern; doch kommen die schlechten Zeiten zu einen Ende, wenn Noel Coward ihn auffordert, als Victor Prynne in der neuen Komodie **Private Lives** aufzutreten, und zwar neben Gertrude Lawrence und Coward selber. Das Stueck wird ein Riesenerfolg, und die Schauspieler ziehen dann damit an den Broadway. Hollywood holt ihn an die Westkueste, speist ihn dann aber zwei Jahre lang mit phantasielosen Rollen ab, so dass er vom Film ganz entäuscht nach London zurueckkehrt.

In England spielt er mit Gloria Swanson in dem Film **Perfect Understanding (Ganz Verstaendig)** und kehrt dann zur West End Buehne zurueck, um mit Ray Massey and Gladys Cooper in **The Rats of Norway (Die Ratten von Norwegen)** aufzutreten. Zurueck nach Hollywood, um mit Garbo in **Queen Christine (Koenigin Christine)** zu spielen. Er findet sich aber durch John Gilbet ersetzt. Dies veranlasst ihn, dem Film seinen Ruecken zuzukehren, und sich ganz dem Theater zu widmen.

Kritiker loben seinen Auftritt in **The Green Bay Trees (Die Gruenen Lorbeer Baeume)** am Broadway. Er geht nach London, um mit Ina Claire in Noel Cowards Auffuehrung von **Biography** zu spielen. In **Mary, Queen of Scots** spielt er Bothwell, und arbeitet hier zum ersten Mal mit John Gielgud zusammen. Es folgt Noel Cowards Auffuehrung des amerikanischen satirischen Stuckes ueber die Barrymore Familie, in welchen Olivier die bombastische Rolle des Matinee Idols 'Tony Cavendish' mit so viel Schwung spielt, dass er sich bei einer Vorstellung, als er vom Balkon springt, einen Knoechel bricht. In **The Ringmaster** spielt er einen neurotischen Invaliden welcher einem Gangster-verband vorsteht.

Es gelingt Alexander Korda, dem ungarischen Filmregisseuren und Hersteller, Olivier von seinem Vorurteil dem Film gegenueber abzubrigen, und Olivier unterzeichnet einen Vertrag mit Korda's Firma, London Films, welche ein eindrucksvolles Programm durchzufuehren gedenkt. Olivier versucht zum ersten Mal seine Hand als Spielleiter mit **Golden Arrow (Der Goldene Pfeil)**, in welchen er mit Greer Garson auftritt. Die hoechste Anerkennung kommt, wenn John Gielgud, unter dessen Regie "Romeo und Julia" (1935) aufgefuehrt wird, sich entschliesst, die ersten sechs Wochen Romeo nicht selber zu spielen, und Olivier bittet, die Rolle zu uebernehmen. Die uebrige Zeit wechseln Gielgud und Olivier zwischen Romeo and Mercutio ab. 1937 ladet Tyrone Guthrie ihn ein, die Titelrolle in einer neuen, ungekuerzten Auffuehrung von **Hamlet** am Old Vic Theater zu spielen. Olivier verbleibt zwei Jahre lang am Old Vic, und spielt in dieser Zeit Macbeth, Henry V, Sir Toby Belch, Jago und Coriolanus.

Hersteller Sam Goldwyn und Filmregisseur William Wyler laden ihn ein, Heathcliff in Emily Brontés **Wuthering Heights** fuer die Leinwand zu spielen, und zwar mit Merle Oberon. Von nun an ist seine Leinwandkarriere positiver. Es folgt die Rolle von Max de Wynter in Hitchcocks Berbeitung von Daphne du Mauriers **Rebecca,** und Mr. Darcy in dem Film von Jane Austens **Pride and Prejudice (Stolz und Vorurteil).** Der zweite Weltkrieg hat begonnen, und er wird als Pilot fuer die Luftwaffe zu See eingezogen. Vorher spielt er noch einen franzoesisch-kanadischen Trapper in **49th Parallel.** Waehrend des Militaerdienstes erhaelt er Urlaub, um in Anthony Asquiths **Demi-Paradise** aufzutreten, in einer Satire ueber einen russischen Ingenieur, der sich im englischen Vorkriegs-Mittelstand verwickelt findet. Spaeter erhält er erneut Urlaub, um **Henry V** zu filmen, welcher Film von Felipe del Guidice finanziert ist. Laurence Olivier unternimmt hier die Riesenaufgabe der Regie, Produktion und Hauptrolle. Zum zweiten Mal bringt er Shakespeare auf die Leinwand (1936 spielt er in Czinner's **As You Like It (Wie es Euch Gefaellt)** mit Elizabeth Bergner) Drehort ist Irland und fuer die langen Trackszenen baut Olivier seinen eigenen Schienenweg. Der Film laeuft elf Monate, und die dreifache Leistung als Regisseur, Produzent und Star bringt Olivier eine spezielle Academy Auszeichnung. Er sagt von der Rolle Henrys: "Die Schwierigkeit bei der Darstellung von Henrys Charackter ist seine Offenheit."

Die Old Vic Truppe stellt die Aktivitaet ein wenn im "Blitz" von London das Theatregebaeude zerstoert wird. Doch schon 1944 gruenden Olivier, Ralph Richardson, Tyrone Guthrie und John Burrell die Gruppe neu, und treten in einem andern Londoner Theater, dem New Theatre, auf. In der ersten Saison spielt er Sergius in **Arms and the Man (Mann und Waffen)** die Titelrolle in **Richard III,** und Astrov in **Uncle Vanya.** Naechste Saison spielt er Hotspur und Shallow in **Henry IV,** Erster und Zweiter Teil, Oedipus in **Oedipus Rex** und Mr. Puff in **The Critic.** Die zwei letzteren Stuecke werden jeweils an einem Abend gegeben. Mit diesem Arrangement faehrt er nach New York. Im gleichen Jahr kehrt er nach London zurueck und spielt Lear in seiner eigenen Produktion von **King Lear.**

Anfangs 1947 begann Olivier an seinem Film **Hamlet** zu arbeiten, in welchem er, wie in **Henry V,** die Regie, Produktion und Titelrolle uebernimmt. Er beschreibt den Film als "eine Studie in **Hamlet,** Tragoedie eines Mannes, der sich nicht entschliessen kann."

"Als ich am **Henry V** arbeitete, dachte ich ueber einen **Hamlet**—Film nach, doch nicht im Konkreten. Als dann ein zweiter Shakespeare Film vorbereitet wurde, war jedoch **Hamlet** die naheliegende Wahl. Meine Erfahrungen mit Henry V hatten mir gezeigt, dass die einzig moegliche Art, **Hamlet** fuer die Leinwand zu bearbeiten, eine wirklich kuehne Adaption des ursprunglichen Schauspiels sei. Ich kann nicht genau festlegen, wann und wie die ersten Ideen fuer die Bearbeitung des Films geboren wurden. Eines Tages waren die letzten Szenen da. Und ich wusste, wie das ganze Konzept des Filmes aufgebaut werden koennte." Er kuerzt das Schauspiel von den ursprünglichen viereinhalb Stunden auf zweieinhalb Stunden im Film, und laesst Rosenkrantz, Gueldenstern und Fortinbras weg. Der Film soll "eine Studie in Hamlet" sein, und nicht ein Film eines notgedrungenerweise gekuerzten klassischen Schauspiels.

Olivier faerbt seine Haare fuer diesen Film, seine Konzeption von Hamlet ist blond. Die Filmarbeit wird mit groesster Sorgfalt vollendet. Das zehnminuetige Duell, zum Beispiel, koestet 14 Tage Arbeit. Waehrend dieser Arbeiten in den Denham Studios erhaelt er die Auszeichnung einer Knighthood in der Birthday Honours List der englischen Koenigin, fuer seinen Beitrag zu Buehne und Leinwand.

Hamlet wird als ein £475,000 Triumph gefeiert. Seine Darstellung wird als grossartig angesehen. Der Film gewinnt den Preis fuer den besten ausländischen Film am Venedig Festival 1948, und auch fuenf Oscars, darunter den fuer den besten Film des Jahres, und den fuer den besten Schauspieler des Jahres.

1948 geht Olivier mit der Old Vic Company auf Tournee nach Australian und Neuseeland, mit **Richard III, By the Skin of Our Teeth (Wir Sind Noch Einmal Davongekommen)** und **School for Scandal (Schule fuer Intrigue).** Er leitet ferner mehrer Stuecke fuer seine eigene Truppe, Laurence Olivier Productions, angefangen mit **Born Yesterday (Von Gestern).** Um seine weitläufigen Plaene als Schauspieler und Intendant zu verwirklichen, mietet er das St. James's Theater und da faehrt er fort, erfahrenen Schauspielern neues Talent zuzugesellen. Eine bis zu der Zeit unbekannte Schauspielerin, Heather Stannard, spielt in Christopher Frys **Venus**

Observed neben Olivier, und gewinnt Ruhm. Peter Finch, welchen Olivier auf seiner Tournee durch Australian als Fabrik-Unterhalter getroffen hatte, wird durch seine Leistung in der wienerischen Rolle in **Daphne Laureola** in den Vorgrund gerueckt. Weitere bemerkenswerte Leistungen Oliviers in jener Zeit sind Menettis Oper **Der Consul, Anthony and Cleopatra** (auch in New York) und **The Sleeping Prince,** welches er einige Jahre spaeter verfilmt.

Obwohl fast ganz mit Theater beschäftigt, findet er Zeit fuer einige Filme, unter anderm William Wyler's **Carrie,** und auch fuer seine erste Sing-Rolle, als der huebsche, furchtlose Strassenräuber in **The Beggar's Opera (Des Bettlers Oper),** Peter Brooks erstem Film als Regisseur.

Dann verbringt er einige Monate mit den Vorbereitungen der Herstellung seines dritten Shakespearefilms, und 1954 dreht er **Richard III,** wiederum haelt er Regie, Produktion und Titelrolle in seinen Haenden, und wiederum sammelt er beruehmte Leute um sich, wie Ralph Richardson, John Gielgud, Claire Bloom, Cedrick Hardwicks, Alec Clunes, Laurence Naismith. Dieser Film wurde in Vistavision gedreht, und die atemberaubenden Schlachtfeldszenen wurden in Spanien gefilmt. Der Film stellt eine grossartige Errungenschaft des engllschen Fllms dar, eine ausserordentliche Leistung eines grossen Schauspielers.

Olivier ueberrascht viele mit der Wahl seines Partners fuer den naechsten Film, wenn er Marlyn Monroe nach Europa holt, um in der Filmbearbeitung von Rattigans **The Sleeping Prince** zu spielen, welches Stueck den neuen Titel **The Prince and the Showgirl** erhaelt. Er entfernt sich von dem klassischen Bild mehr, als er es uebernimmt, als der fadenscheinige, heruntergekommene Music-Hall Artist Archie Rice in John Osborne's **The Entertainer (Der Unterhalter)** zuerst auf der Buehne, und dann auch in Tony Richardson's Filmversion mit Albert Finney in einer Nebenrolle, aufzutreten.

Olivier versucht, die nötigen £500,000 fuer eine Verfilmung von **Macbeth** zu erhalten. Er koennte die Summe erhalten, verpflichtete er sich, in einer Bearbeitung fuer die Beuhne des Buches **Jane Eyre** aufzutreten. Er entschliesst sich aber fuer die Rolle von General Burgoyne in dem Film von Shaws **The Devil's Disciple (Des Teufels Schueler)** in welchem er neben Burt Lancaster spielt. Es folgt sein Debut am britischen Fernsehen, in **John Gabriel Borkman,** doch sieht er dies als eine Katastrophe an. Es geht ihm etwas besser am amerikanischen Fernsehn, in dem Stück **The Moon and Sixpence (Der Mond und Groschen)** "keine Katastrophe, es gewann sogar einen kleinen Oscar" sagt er. Dann kehrt er nach Hollywood zurück, und spielt dort mit Kirk Douglas und Charles Laughton in Stanley Kubricks Film ueber politische Intrige, **Spartacus.**

Olivier testet seine Kraefte zum äussersten, wenn er Coriolanus in Stratford-on-Avon mit Erscheinen vor den Kameras im **Entertainer** verbindet. Er schlaeft waehrend dieser Zeit in einer Amulanz, die ihn von Stratford an den Drehort nach Norden faehrt. Es folgt **The Tumbler** auf einer New York Buehne, **The Rhinoceros (Die Nashoerner)** in London. 1960, wiederum in New York, die erfolgreiche Auffuehrung von **Becket,** in welcher er mit Anthony Quinn in den Rollen Henry II und Becket abwechselt. In New York spielt er auch in David Susskinds Bearbeitung fuer das Fernsehn von **The Power and the Glory (Macht und Ruhm),** mit Julie Harris und George C. Scott, welcher Film in Europa in den Kinos gezeigt wird. Zurueck in England gruendet er das Chichester Festival Theatre, und spielt die Hauptrolle in Peter Glenvilles **Term of Trial (Zeitpunkt der Spannung),** mit Simone Signoret, Terence Stamp, und Sarah Miles.

Im August 1962 uebernimmt er die Leitung des National Theatres, welches mit seiner Produktion von **Hamlet** oeffnet, Peter O'Toole in der Titelrolle. Er traegt viel zu dem Erfolg des National Theatres bei mit seinen Auftritten in **Othello, Uncle Vanya, The Recruiting Officer** und **The Master Builder (Der Baumeister).** Die Truppe tourniert in England, besucht Moskau und Westberlin, mit Oliviers **Othello** in Zentrum.

1965 wird eines der aktivsten Jahre seiner Karriere. Vier neue Produktionen des National Theatres, John Ardens **Armstrong's Last Goodnight,** Pineros **Trelawney of the Wells,** die Doppelnummer von Strindbergs **Miss Julie (Fraulein Julie)** und Peter Shaffers **Black Comedy (Schwarze Komoedie)** und Congreves **Love for Love,** in welchem er Tattle spielt. Neben diesen Arbeiten dreht er seinen ersten Film in vier Jahren. Er stellt seine ganze Zeiteinteilung um, um in Premingers **Bunny Lake is Missing (Bunny Lake wird Vermisst)** den Scotland Yard Inspektor zu spielen, der das mysteriöse Verschwinden eines Kindes in London untersucht. Dieser Film bringt ihn wiederum mit jenem Mann zusammen, der ihm vor fünfunddreissig Jahren den Durchbruch auf der Londoner Buehe ermoeglicht hat, naemlich Noel Coward. Im gleichen Jahr beginnt die Filmproduktion von **Othello,** mit den gleichen Schauspielern wie auf der Buehne. Er sagt von dem Film, es solle weder ein eigentlicher Film, noch eine blosse Aufzeichnung der Auffuehrung sein.

Ein dritter Film folgt im gleichen Jahr, wenn er den fanatischen Mahdi in Basil Dreardons **Khartoum** spielt, mit Charles Heston als General Gordon und Ralph Richardson as Gladstone.

Obwohl immer mehr mit Administration beschaeftigt, findet er Zeit, neues Talent zu entdecken und zu fördern, und auch die Schauspielerinnen und Schauspieler des National Theatres, sowie auch das Publikum, weiterhin mit seiner Originalitaet und Kraft zu erstaunen, welche er jedem neuen Auftritt zugrundelegt.

FILMOGRAPHY

d	Director: Metteur en scène: Régisseur
p	Producer: Producteur: Produktionsleitung
P	Production; Production; Produktion
s	Script: Scenario: Drehbuch
f	Director of Photography: Chef opérateur: Chef-Kameramann
m	Music: musique: Musik
a	Costumes/Design: Decors/Costumes: Architekt, Inszenant
C	Cast: Interpretation: Darsteller

THE TEMPORARY WIDOW
1930
Germany: U.K.
P   U.F.A.
d   G. Ucicky
C   Laurence Olivier, Lilian Harvey, Felix Aylmer, Frederick Lloyd

TOO MANY CROOKS
1930
U.K.
P   Twentieth Century Fox
d   George King
C   Dorothy Boyd, Bromley Davenport, Arthur Stratton

THE YELLOW PASSPORT (THE YELLOW TICKET)
1931
U.S.A.
P   Twentieth Century Fox
d   Raoul Walsh
s   Michael Morton
C   Elissa Landi, Lionel Barrymore, Boris Karloff

FRIENDS AND LOVERS
1931
U.S.A.
P   R.K.O.
d   Victor Schertzinger
s   Maurice de Kobra
C   Adolphe Menjou, Lily Damita, Erich von Stroheim.

POTIPHAR'S WIFE
1931
U.K.
d   Maurice Elvey
s   Edgar Middleton
C   Norah Swinburne, Guy Newall, Norman McKinnell

WESTWARD PASSAGE
1932
U.S.A.
d   Robert Milton
P   R.K.O.
s   Margaret Barnes
C   Ann Harding, Zasu Pitts, Juliette Compton

THE PERFECT UNDERSTANDING
1932
U.K.
d   Cyril Gardner
C   Gloria Swanson, John Halliday

NO FUNNY BUSINESS
1933
U.K.
d   John Stafford and Victor Hanbury
p   John Stafford
C   Gertrude Lawrence, Jill Esmond, Gib McLaughlin, Edmond Breon

MOSCOW NIGHTS
1935
U.K.
d   Anthony Asquith
P   Denham
p   Alexis Granowsky
s   Eric Siepmann
f   Phillip Tannura
C   Ignatoff . . . . Laurence Olivier
       Brionkow . . . . Harry Baur
       Natasha . . . . Penelope Dudley Ward

AS YOU LIKE IT
1936
U.K.
P   Inter-Allied Film Producers Ltd.
dp   Paul Czinner
f   Hal Rosson
m   William Walton
s   William Shakespeare
a   John Armstrong and Joe Strassner
C   Rosalind . . . . Elisabeth Bergner
       Orlando . . . . Laurence Olivier
       Celia . . . . . Sophie Stewart
       Exiled Duke . . . Henry Ainley
       Jaques . . . . . Leon Quartermaine
       Duke Frederick . . Felix Aylmer

FIRE OVER ENGLAND
1937
U.K.
d   William K. Howard
s   Clemence Dane and Sergei Noibanov from the novel by A. E. W. Mason
f   James Wong Howe
P   Pendennis
C   Vivien Leigh, Leslie Banks, Flora Robson, Raymond Bassey, Morton Selten, Tamara Desni, Lyn Harding, George Thirlwell

THE DIVORCE OF LADY X
1938
U.K.
d   Tim Whelan
P   London Films
p   Alexander Korda
f   Harry Stradling
m   Miklos Rosza
93 mins.
C   Merle Oberon, Binnie Barnes, Ralph Richardson

CONQUEST OF THE AIR
1938
U.K.
d   Alexander Shaw
p   Donald Taylow
P   London Films
C   Lunardi   . . . . Laurence Olivier
       Isobella d'Est . . . Margaretta Scott

Q PLANES
1938
U.K.
d   Tim Whelan
P   London Films International Ltd.
p   Irving Asher
s   Ian Dalrymple
C   Laurence Olivier, Ralph Richardson, Valerie Hobson

TWENTY ONE DAYS (THE FIRST AND THE LAST)
1939
U.K.
dp	Basil Dean
s	Graham Greene and Basil Dean from John Galsworthy's "The First and The Last"
f	Jan Stallich
C	Laurence Olivier . Larry Darrant
	Vivien Leigh . . . Wanda
	& Leslie Banks, Frances Sullivan, Hay Petrie, Robert Newton & Esme Percy

WUTHERING HEIGHTS
1939
U.S.A.
d	William Wyler
p	Sam Goldwyn
P	New Realm Pictures Ltd.
s	Ben Hecht & Charles MacArthur
f	Gregg Toland
m	Alfred Newman
C	Heathcliff . . . Laurence Olivier
	Cathy . . . . . Merle Oberon
	Edgar . . . . . David Niven
	Ellen Dean . . . Flora Robson

REBECCA
U.S.A.
1940
U.S.A.
d	Alfred Hitchcock
P	David O. Selznick Productions
s	Robert E. Sherwood & Joan Harrison from novel by Daphne du Maurier
f	George Barnes
C	Joan Fontaine, George Sanders, Judith Anderson, Gladys Cooper

PRIDE AND PREJUDICE
1941
U.S.A.
d   Robert Z. Leonard
p   Hunt Stromberg
s   Aldous Huxley and Jane Murfin
m   Herbert Stothart
f   Karl Frenn A.S.C.
C   Greer Garson, Mary Boland, Edna May Olivier, Maureen O'Sullivan, Ann Rutherford

LADY HAMILTON
1941
U.K.
P   London Films International Ltd.
pd   Alexander Korda
m   Miklos Rozsa
s   Walter Reisch, R. C. Sherriff
f   Rudolph Mate
C   Nelson   . . . . Laurence Olivier
      Emma . . . . . . Vivien Leigh

49th PARALLEL
U.K.
P   General Film Distributors Ltd.
pd   Michael Powell
s   Rodney Ackland and Emeric Pressburger
f   Frederick Young
m   Vaughan Williams
Editor   David Lean
C   Eric Portman

THE DEMI-PARADISE
1943
U.K.
d   Anthony Asquith
P   Two Cities
ps   Anatole de Grunwald
p   Bernard Knowles
m   Nicholas Brodsky
C   Laurence Olivier as Ivan Dimitrievitch Kouznetsoff, and Penelope Ward, Marjorie Fielding, Margaret Rutherford, Felix Aylmer

34

HENRY Vth
1945
U.K.
dp   Laurence Olivier
s   Laurence Olivier, Allen Dent from William Shakespeare
f   Robert Krasker
m   Sir William Walton
a   Carmen Dillon, Paul Sheriff, Robert Fierse
C   Renee Asherson, Ivy St. Helier

HAMLET
1947/8
U.K.
dp   Laurence Olivier
s   William Shakespeare
P   Two Cities for Rank
m   Sir William Walton
f   Desmond Dickinson
a   Roger Ramsdell
C   Laurence Olivier . Hamlet
     Jean Simmons . . Ophelia
     Eileen Herlie . . . Queen
     Basil Sydney . . King
     Norman Woolland . Horatio
     Felix Aylmer . . Polonius
     Terence Morgan . . Laertes

CARRIE
1952
U.S.A.
dp   William Wyler
P   Paramount
s   Ruth & Augustus Goetz from Theodore Dreiser's "Sister Carrie".
121 mins.
C   George Hurstwood . Laurence Olivier
     Carrie Meeber . . Jennifer Jones
     Julia Hurstwood . Miriam Hopkins
     Charles Drouet . . Eddie Albert

THE BEGGAR'S OPERA
1952
U.K.

d	Peter Brook
P	British Lion Film Corporation
p	Laurence Olivier & Herbert Wilcox
s	Denis Cannan, Christopher Fry
m	Sir Arthur Bliss
f	Guy Green (Technicolor)
a	George Wakhevitch, William C. Andrews

94 mins.

C	Captain Macheath .	Laurence Olivier
	Lockit	Stanley Holloway
	Peachum	George Devine
	Mrs. Peachum . .	Mary Clare
	Mrs. Trapes . .	Athene Seyler
	Polly Peachum . .	Dorothy Tutin
	Lucy Lockit . . .	Daphne Anderson
	The Beggar . . .	Hugh Griffith
	The ◆Actress . . .	Margot Grahame
	The Footman . . .	Denis Cannan

RICHARD THE THIRD
1955
U.K.

d	Laurence Olivier
P	London Films and Laurence Olivier Productions
f	Otto Heller (Vistavision EastmanColour)
s	William Shakespeare/Alan Dent
m	Sir William Walton
a	Roger Furse

160 mins.

C	Richard III	Laurence Olivier
	Buckingham . . .	Ralph Richardson
	Clarence	John Gielgud
	Lady Anne . . .	Claire Bloom
	Edward IV	Cedric Hardwicke
	Richmond . . .	Stanley Baker
	Hastings	Alec Clunes

THE PRINCE AND THE SHOWGIRL
1956
U.K.
dp   Laurence Olivier
P   Laurence Olivier Productions for Warner Brothers
      (Pinewood)
s   Terence Rattigan from his play "The Sleeping Prince"
f   Jack Cardiff (Technicolor)
a   Carmen Dillon
116 mins.

C		
The Regent	. . .	Laurence Olivier
Elise	. . . . .	Marilyn Monroe
Queen Dowager	.	Sybil Thorndike
Northbrook	. . .	Richard Wattis
King Nicholas	. .	Jeremy Spenser

THE DEVIL'S DISCIPLE
1958
U.K.
d   Guy Hamilton
p   Harold Hecht
s   John Dighton & Roland Kibbee, from play by Bernard
      Shaw
f   Jack Hildyard
m   Richard Rodney Bennett
P   United Artists
83 mins.

C		
Pastor Anderson	.	Burt Lancaster
Richard Dudgeon	.	Kirk Douglas
General Burgoyne	.	Laurence Olivier
Judith	. . . .	Janette Scott
Major Swindon	. .	Harry Andrews

THE MOON AND SIXPENCE
1959   U.S.A. Television
p   David Susskind
d   Robert Mulligan
s   S. Lee Pogostin from W. Somerset Maughan
90 mins.
C   Laurence Olivier, Judith Anderson, Hume Cronyn,
     Jessica Tandy, Geraldine Fitzgerald, Denholm Elliot,
     Jean March, Cyril Cusak, Murray Matheson

SPARTACUS
1959   U.S.A.
d   Stanley Kubrick
p   Edward Lewis
s   Dalton Trumbo from novel by Howard Fast
f   Russell Metty
m   Alex North
P   Bryna Production for Universal International
Technicolor: Super Technirama: 193 mins.
C   Spartacus . . . . Kirk Douglas
     Marcus Crassus . Laurence Olivier
     Varinia . . . . . Jean Simmons
     Gracchus . . . . Charles Laughton
     Batiatus . . . . Peter Ustinov
     Julius Caesar . . John Gavin
     Antonius . . . . Tony Curtis

THE ENTERTAINER
1960   U.K.
d   Tony Richardson
p   Harry Saltzman
s   John Osborne & Nigel Kneale
f   Oswald Morris
m   John Addison
P   Woodfall Production distributed by British Lion
104 mins.
C   Archie Rice . . . Laurence Olivier
     Phoebe Rice . . . Brenda de Banzie
     Jean . . . . . Joan Plowright
     Billy . . . . . Roger Livesey
     Frank . . . . . Alan Bates
     Graham . . . . Daniel Massey
     Mick Rice . . . . Albert Finney

THE POWER AND THE GLORY
1961
U.S.A. (Television)
P	Paramount Pictures Corporation		
d	Marc Daniels		
s	Dale Wasserman from novel by Graham Greene		
p	David Susskind		
C	The Priest	. . .	Laurence Olivier
	Marie	. . . . .	Julie Harris
	Police Lieutenant	.	George C. Scott
	Peasant	. . . .	Roddy McDowall
	Bootlegger	. . .	Keenan Wynn

TERM OF TRIAL
1962
U.K.
d	Peter Glenville		
p	James Woolf		
P	Romulus Films for Warner Brothers		
s	Peter Glenville from novel by James Barlow		
f	Oswald Morris		

130 mins.
C	Graham Weir	. .	Laurence Olivier
	Anna	. . . . .	Simone Signoret
	Shirley Taylor	. .	Sarah Miles
	O'Harum	. . . .	Hugh Griffith
	Mitchell	. . . .	Terence Stamp

BUNNY LAKE IS MISSING
1965
U.K.
dp	Otto Preminger	
s	John & Penelope Mortimer from novel by Evelyn Waugh	
f	Denys Coop	
P	Columbia Pictures Corporation	

107 mins.
C	Steven	. . . .	Keir Dullea
	Ann	. . . . .	Carol Lynley
	Newhouse	. . .	Laurence Olivier
	Wilson	. . . .	Noel Coward
	Elvira	. . . . .	Anna Massey

OTHELLO
1965
U.K.

d   Stuart Burge
p   Anthony Havelock-Allan & John Brabourne
P   BHE Production through Eagle Films Ltd.
a   Jocelyn Herbert & William Kellner
f   Geoffrey Unsworth (Panavision & Technicolor)
C   The Moor . . . . Laurence Olivier
      Desdemona . . . Maggie Smith
      Emelia . . . . . Joyce Redman
      Iago . . . . . Frank Finlay
      Cassio . . . . Derek Jacobi
      Roderigo . . . . Robert Lang

KHARTOUM
1966
U.K.

d   Basil Dearden
p   Julian Blaustein
s   Robert Ardrey
f   Ted Scaife
P   United Artists
C   The Mahdi . . . . Laurence Olivier
      General Gordon . . Charlton Heston
      Col. Stewart . . . Richard Johnson
      Gladstone . . . Ralph Richardson

2

AS YOU LIKE IT

I think the King is but a man as I am.

And what have kings that privates have not too,
Save ceremony—

From this day to the ending of the world,
But we in it shall be remembered—
We few, we happy few, we band of brothers ;

For he today that sheds his blood with me
Shall be my brother ;

and that this day shall change all griefs and
quarrels into love.

He that outlives this day, and comes safe home,
Will stand tip-toe when this day is nam'd,
And rouse him at the name of Crispian.

Dat it is not be de fashion pour le ladies
of France—I cannot tell vat is baiser
en Anglish.

—and you may, some of you, thank love for my
blindness, who cannot see many a fair French city
for one fair french maid that stands in my way.

HAMLET

PRINCE OF DENMARK

And for my soul, what can it do to that,
Being a thing immortal as itself ?
It waves me forth again ; I'll follow it.

Is this a prologue, or the posy of a ring?
'Tis brief my lord.
As woman's love.

Go to, I'll no more on't;
it hath made me mad.

Now get you to my lady's chamber, and tell her, let
her paint an inch thick, to this favour she must come
make her laugh at that.

How came he mad ?
Very strangely, they say.

A villain kills my father : and for that
I, his sole son, do this same
villain send to heaven.

Thou wretched, rash, intruding fool, farewell.

But look, amazement on thy mother sits.
O, step between her and her fighting soul !
Conceit in weakest bodies strongest works.

Nymph, in thy orisons,
Be all my sins rememb'red.

KING RICHARD THE THIRD

Alack, I love myself. Wherefore? For any good
That I myself have done unto myself?
O, no! Alas, I rather hate myself
For hateful deeds committed by myself!
I am a villain; yet I lie, I am not.

What though I kill'd her husband and her father ?
The readiest way to make amends
Is to become her husband and her father.

And therefore, since I cannot prove a lover
To entertain these fair well-spoken days,
I am determined to prove a villain
And hate the idle pleasures of these days.

Slave, I have set my life upon a cast
And I will stand the hazard of the die.
I think there be six Richmonds in the field ;
Five have I slain today instead of him.
A horse ! a horse ! my kingdom for a horse !

OTHELLO

THE MOOR OF VENICE

Come, my dear love,
The purchase made, the fruits are to ensue ;
That profit's yet to come twixt me and you.

I will deny thee nothing.
Whereon I do beseech thee grant me this,
To leave me but a little to myself.

What voice is this ? Not dead ? not
yet quite dead ?
I that am cruel am yet merciful ;
I would not have thee linger in thy pain.

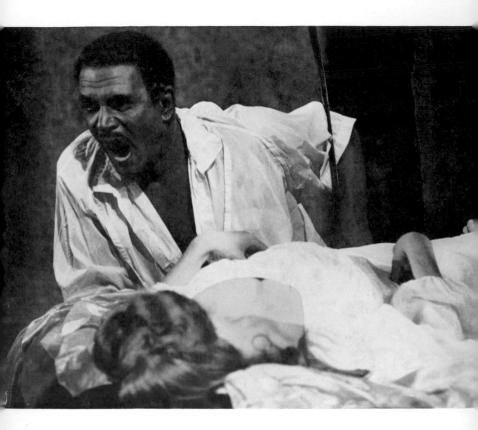

O cursed, cursed slave !
Whip me, ye devils,
From the possession of this heavenly sight.
Blow me about in winds, roast me in sulphur,
Wash me in steep-down gulfs of liquid fire.

I kiss'd thee ere I kill'd thee.
No way but this—
Killing my self, to die upon a kiss.